INDY CARS

BY DENNY VON FINN

150

160

70

TORQUE
TM

BELLWETHER MEDIA • MINNEAPOLIS, MN

Are you ready to take it to the extreme?
Torque books thrust you into the action-packed world
of sports, vehicles, and adventure. These books may
include dirt, smoke, fire, and dangerous stunts.
WARNING: read at your own risk.

This edition first published in 2011 by Bellwether Media, Inc.

No part of this publication may be reproduced in whole or in part without written permission of the publisher.
For information regarding permission, write to Bellwether Media, Inc., Attention: Permissions Department,
5357 Penn Avenue South, Minneapolis, MN 55419.

Library of Congress Cataloging-in-Publication Data

Von Finn, Denny.
Indy cars / by Denny Von Finn.
    p. cm. -- (Torque: The world's fastest)
 Includes bibliographical references and index.
Summary: "Amazing photography accompanies engaging information about Indy cars. The combination
of high-interest subject matter and light text is intended for students in grades 3 through 7"--Provided by
publisher.
ISBN 978-1-60014-588-9 (hardcover : alk. paper)
1. Indy cars--Juvenile literature. I. Title.
TL236.V655 2010
796.72--dc22   2010034746

Printed in the United States of America, North Mankato, MN.

010111   1176

CONTENTS

What Are Indy Cars?

Indy cars are **open-wheel race cars**. This means their wheels are located outside of their bodies. Open-wheel race cars are lightweight and built for speed. An Indy car can reach speeds of more than 220 miles (354 kilometers) per hour.

Fast Fact

In 1996, driver Paul Tracy recorded one of the fastest Indy car speeds ever. He reached 257 miles (414 kilometers) per hour while speeding around the track!

Fast Fact

The IRL awards points for a driver's finish in each race. The better the finish, the more points a driver receives. At the end of the year, the driver with the most points wins the IRL championship.

Indy cars race in the **Indy Racing League (IRL)**. The IRL hosts several races each season. Most Indy car races take place in the United States. Some Indy car races are held on oval-shaped tracks. Other races are on **road courses**.

Indy car races are long. They range from 200 to 500 miles (322 to 805 kilometers). One of these races is the Indianapolis 500. This is the world's most famous automobile race.

Fast Fact

It is tradition for the winner of the Indianapolis 500 to drink from a bottle of milk in the winner's circle.

The first Indianapolis 500 was held in 1911. Today, around 400,000 people attend the race each year.

Indy Car Technology

roll hoop

Many high-tech parts help an Indy car reach its fast speeds. These parts also help drivers handle the cars on both oval tracks and twisting road courses. The **chassis** is the base of an Indy car. This frame is made of **carbon fiber**. The **roll hoop** is an important part of the chassis. It protects the driver inside the **cockpit** if the car rolls over.

wings

Wide tires and two **wings** help an Indy car stay on the track during a race. The wings are attached to the front and back of the chassis. Air rushes over the wings to create **downforce**. The rushing wind pushes the car down to the track. The smooth tires heat up as they roll over the pavement. They become sticky and grip the track.

Fast Fact

An Indy car's gas tank is made of rubber and covered with a high-strength material called Kevlar. This Kevlar "blanket" provides protection in case of crashes.

An Indy car needs a powerful engine to compete in the IRL. A **V-8** engine has eight **cylinders** and sends power to the wheels. The engine is attached to the chassis and sits behind the driver. Today's Indy car engines can create 670 **horsepower**. That's more than three times as powerful as a normal car engine!

Fast Fact

Early Indy cars had their engines mounted in front of the driver.

V-8 engine

The Future of Indy Cars

Racing an Indy car is expensive. A single car uses more than 250 gallons (946 liters) of fuel during the Indianapolis 500!

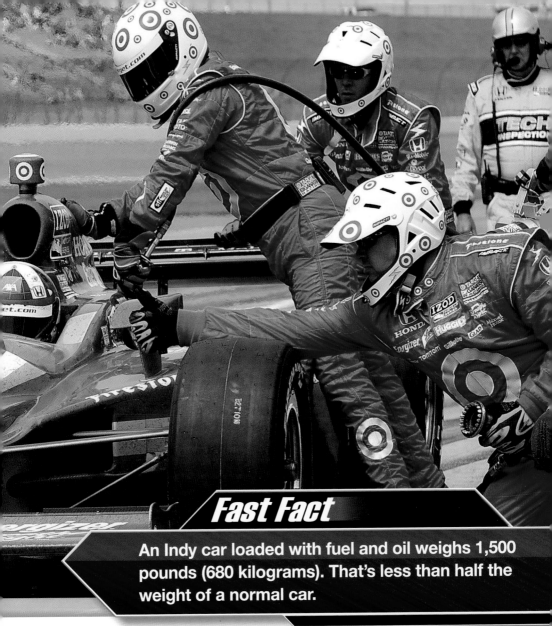

An Indy car loaded with fuel and oil weighs 1,500 pounds (680 kilograms). That's less than half the weight of a normal car.

One way to decrease fuel use is to make the cars weigh less. Lighter cars need less power and less fuel. This means that future Indy cars could have smaller engines and still be as fast as today's Indy cars.

Car companies are interested in making engines that use less fuel. They are building Indy car engines with only four or six cylinders. Some race teams believe the IRL should let them **tune** these smaller engines. This means the teams could adjust them for the demands of different Indy race tracks.

Fast Fact

Danica Patrick is today's top female Indy car driver. Patrick, Simona de Silvestro, Sarah Fisher, and Janet Guthrie have helped open the sport to women.

The IRL is trying to build safer Indy cars. Future
Indy cars will have improved wings. These will create
more downforce to help the cars grip the track.

Design changes will also help prevent an Indy car's exposed wheels from touching another car's wheels. Wheel contact is a leading cause of crashes. Fewer crashes will help ensure that fans enjoy the high-speed thrills of Indy car racing for years to come.

GLOSSARY

carbon fiber—a strong material made by covering fabric with plastic

chassis—the frame on which a vehicle is built

cockpit—the area in an Indy car where the driver sits

cylinders—hollow chambers inside an engine in which fuel is burned to create power

downforce—a physical force that pushes a car down to the track; lightweight Indy cars need downforce to stay on the track at high speeds.

horsepower—a unit used to measure the power of an engine

Indy Racing League (IRL)—the league that organizes and hosts Indy car races

open-wheel race cars—cars with wheels located outside of their bodies

road courses—race tracks that feature both left and right turns

roll hoop—the part of an Indy car chassis that protects the driver in case of a rollover

tune—to adjust an engine for maximum performance

V-8—an engine that has two sides of four slanted cylinders that form a "V" shape

wings—flat metal surfaces attached to the front and back of an Indy car to create downforce

TO LEARN MORE

AT THE LIBRARY

David, Jack. *Indy Cars*. Minneapolis, Minn.: Bellwether Media, 2008.

McCollum, Sean. *Indy Cars*. Mankato, Minn.: Capstone Press, 2010.

Pimm, Nancy Roe. *Indy 500: The Inside Track*. Plain City, Ohio: Darby Creek Pub., 2004.

ON THE WEB

Learning more about Indy cars is as easy as 1, 2, 3.

1. Go to www.factsurfer.com.

2. Enter "Indy cars" into the search box.

3. Click the "Surf" button and you will see a list of related Web sites.

With factsurfer.com, finding more information is just a click away.

INDEX

The images in this book are reproduced through the courtesy of: Gavin Lawrence/Stringer/Getty Images, front cover, pp. 4-5, 12-13; Robert Laberge/Stringer/Getty Images, pp. 6-7, 9; Nick Laham/Getty Images, p. 8; Gerardo Burgos Galindo, pp. 10-11; Domenic Gareri, pp. 14-15; Transtock Inc./Alamy, p. 15 (small); Rick Dole/Stringer/Getty Images, pp. 16-17; Christian Petersen/Getty Images, pp. 18-19; Walter G. Arce, p. 19 (small); LatinContent/Getty Images, pp. 20-21.